Boogers and Snot

by Grace Hansen

Abdo
Kids

BEGINNING SCIENCE:
GROSS BODY FUNTIONS

Abdo Kids Jumbo is an Imprint of Abdo Kids
abdobooks.com

abdobooks.com

Published by Abdo Kids, a division of ABDO, P.O. Box 398166, Minneapolis, Minnesota 55439.
Copyright © 2021 by Abdo Consulting Group, Inc. International copyrights reserved in all countries.
No part of this book may be reproduced in any form without written permission from the publisher.
Abdo Kids Jumbo™ is a trademark and logo of Abdo Kids.

Printed in the United States of America, North Mankato, Minnesota.

052020
092020

 THIS BOOK CONTAINS
RECYCLED MATERIALS

Photo Credits: Alamy, iStock, Science Source, Shutterstock

Production Contributors: Teddy Borth, Jennie Forsberg, Grace Hansen
Design Contributors: Dorothy Toth, Pakou Moua

Library of Congress Control Number: 2019956464
Publisher's Cataloging-in-Publication Data

Names: Hansen, Grace, author.

Title: Boogers and snot / by Grace Hansen

Description: Minneapolis, Minnesota : Abdo Kids, 2021 | Series: Beginning science: gross body functions |
    Includes online resources and index.

Identifiers: ISBN 9781098202354 (lib. bdg.) | ISBN 9781644943823 (pbk.) | ISBN 9781098203337 (ebook)
    | ISBN 9781098203825 (Read-to-Me ebook)

Subjects: LCSH: Human body--Juvenile literature. | Nasal mucosa--Juvenile literature. | Body fluids--
    Juvenile literature. | Excretion--Juvenile literature. | Hygiene--Juvenile literature.

Classification: DDC 612--dc23

Table of Contents

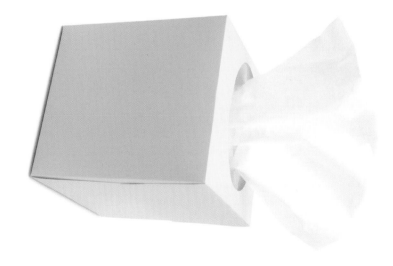

Let's Boogie!

Boogers and snot can be
pretty gross! But they actually
have an important job to do
inside your body.

4

trapped germ

mucus

17

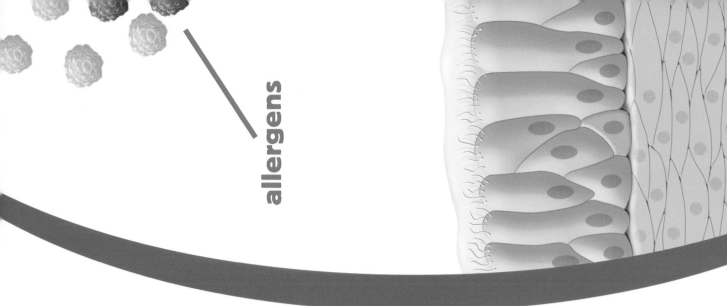

allergens

If you are sick or have allergies, you might have to blow your nose a lot. You also might feel **inflammation**. This is your body's way of reacting to and flushing allergens out.

18

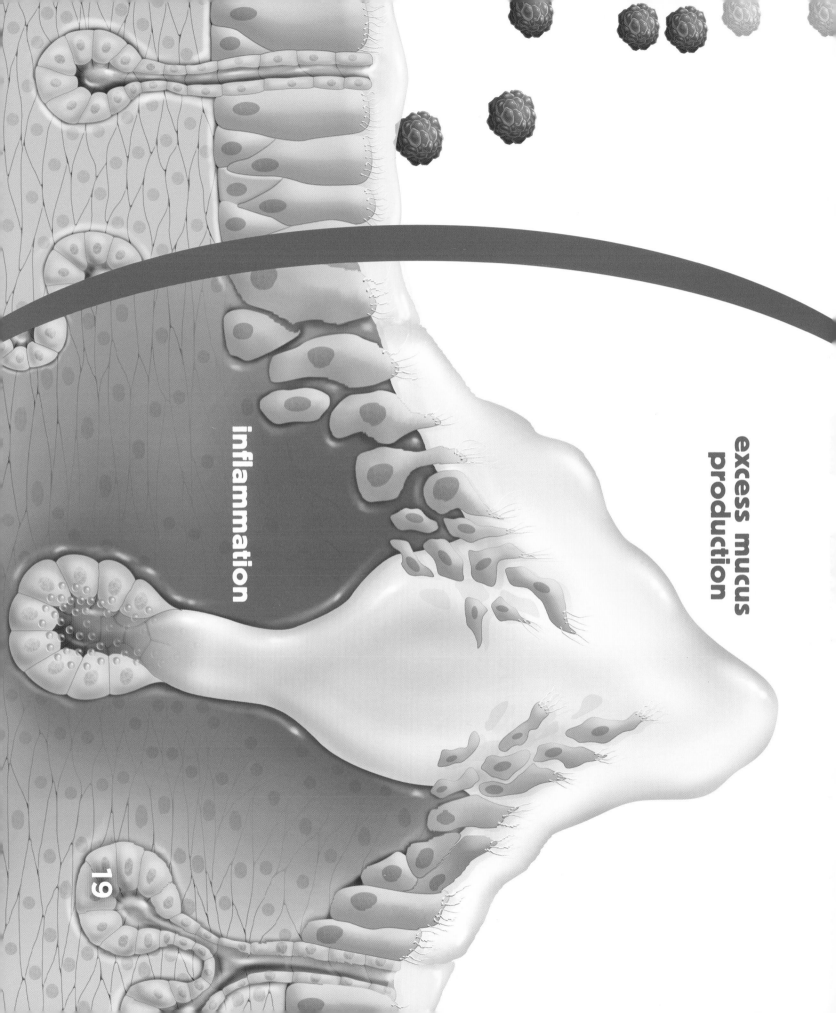

inflammation

excess mucus production

19

Sometimes you even cough up **mucus**. This is just another way the body gets rid of germs or irritants!

20

Let's Review!

- Snot is mucus. A booger is dried mucus.

- Mucous membranes make mucus. These membranes line the mouth, nose, lungs, and other areas of the body.

- Mucus production is part of our innate immune system.

- The immune system protects us from germs that enter our bodies.

- Mucus is thick and sticky. It traps germs. Then the mucus leaves our bodies through the nostrils or mouth.

Glossary

allergy – a condition in which a person's body has an unusual reaction to certain things.

antibody – a protein that reacts to particular toxic substances by neutralizing or destroying them.

inflammation – a physical condition in which an area of the body becomes swollen, hot, and red as a reaction to injury or infection.

innate – existing in someone from the time of birth.

mucus – a slimy, slightly sticky material that coats and protects certain parts of the body.

protein – a substance found in all living things that is a necessary part of life processes.

Index

Abdo Kids
ONLINE
FREE! ONLINE MULTIMEDIA RESOURCES

Visit abdokids.com to access crafts, games, videos, and more!

Use Abdo Kids code

BBK2354

or scan this QR code!

Snot is another word for **mucus**

that comes out of the nose.

Boogers are dried snot.

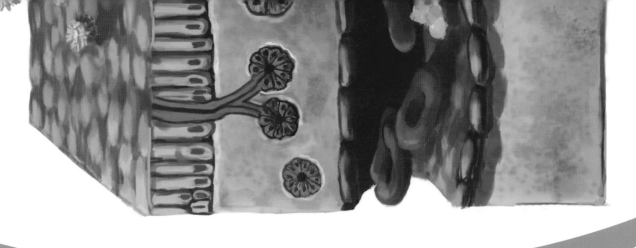

Making Mucus

Mucous membranes make mucus. Mucous membranes are a part of your innate immune system. Your immune system helps fight germs that enter your body.

germs & viruses

mucous gland

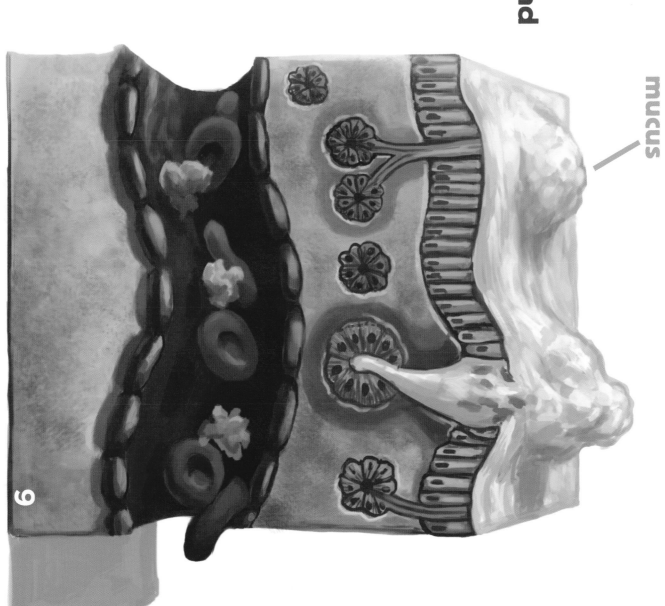

mucus

6

Mucous membranes line the inside of the nose and mouth. They also line the lungs and other areas of the body.

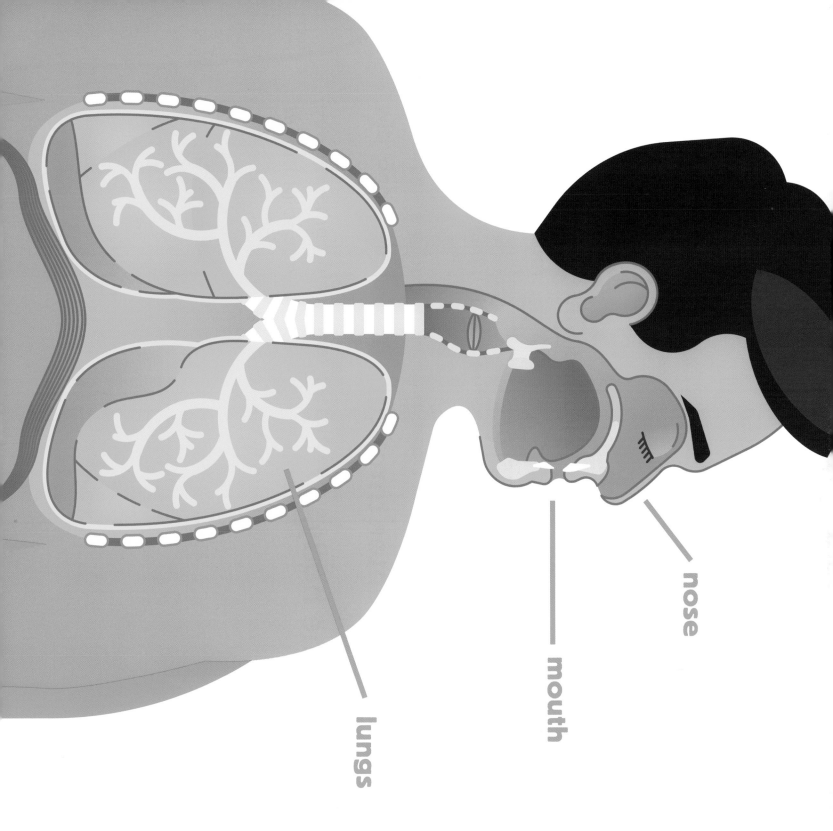

lungs

mouth

nose

The nose, mouth, and lungs are open to the outside world. It is easy for germs to enter through these parts of the body.

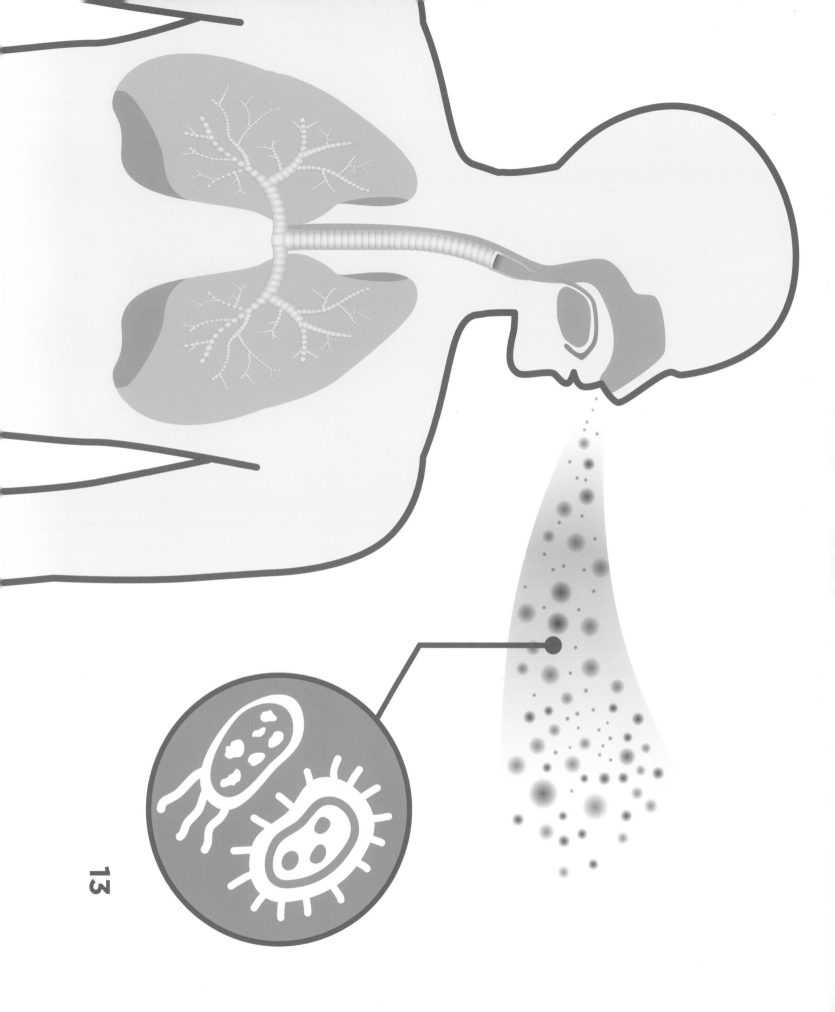

Mucus is mostly made up of water and salt. But it also has proteins and antibodies. These things help fight germs.

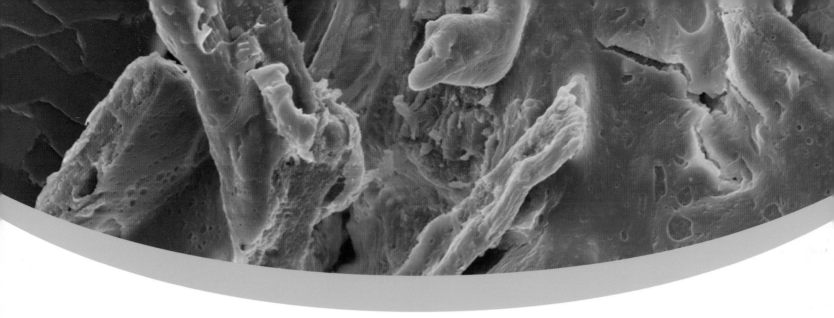

Mucus is also thick and sticky. This helps it to trap germs.